rugby
THE DICTIONARY

British Library Cataloguing in Publication Data

Webster, Jim
    Rugby: the dictionary.
    1. Rugby football—Anecdotes, facetiae, satire, etc.
    I. Title
    796.33'3'0207   GV945.2

    ISBN 0-7153-8764-2

First published in Australia by Sun Books 1985
First published in the United Kingdom by David & Charles 1985

Printed in Great Britain
by Butler & Tanner, Frome and London
for David & Charles (Publishers) Limited
Brunel House   Newton Abbot   Devon

rugby

THE DICTIONARY
BY JIM WEBSTER
ILLUSTRATED BY BILL MITCHELL

DAVID & CHARLES

Newton Abbot   London

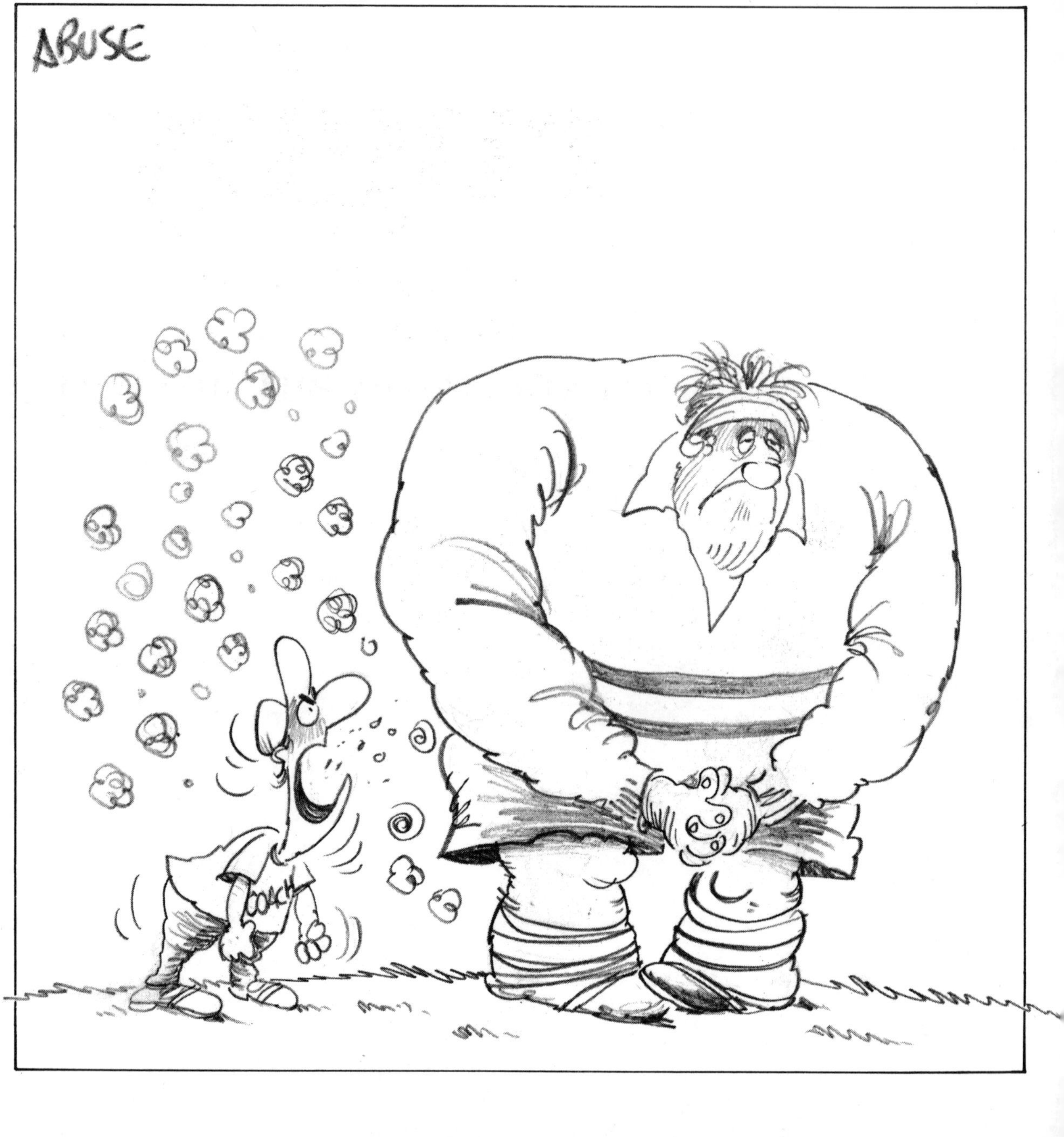
ABUSE
COACH

A

Abuse	Turns defeat into victory.
Advantage	The advantage law is more often applied when the referee wants a date with your captain's sister.
After-Match Functions	The officials take over from the players and hand out ties and make speeches to which the players don't listen.
All Blacks	Unsavoury types. They've largely pilfered Rugby from the Poms. The name and uniform symbolize their opponents' deep depression.

ALL BLACK

Arms Park   A sacred site in Wales for visiting Australians since 24 November, 1984. Any Rugby player who has lost a limb in battle can store it here for safe-keeping.

ARMS PARK

Arthritis	An affliction normally developed late in one's playing career and attacking the right elbow. Medical opinion suggests that drinking through a straw would otherwise prevent it.
Autobiography	Mandatory for famous players on retirement. Contains photograph of said hero in short pants as well as one of wife and family, criticism of officials, a World XV in which he selects himself, a tit-bit of sensationalism to assist the sales and a neat list of figures at the end of the book detailing his career stats. Makes an excellent door-stopper.

AUTOGRAPH

Autograph	A star player practising to become illegible. Many of them become doctors.
Aye	As in 'Aye ref, what's that flippin' penalty for?'

B

Ball Boy	The boy on the touch-line with balls under each arm.
Bandage	As common in Rugby as talkative half-backs. Never worn on the knee which actually hurts, but on the 'good' knee so as to fool any opposing players who might have evil intent. This means that the 'bad' knee has no support and therefore never gets better.
Beer	Persistent rumours suggest that the brewers of this amber fluid actually conceived the game of Rugby football and not William Webb Ellis at all.

Best and Fairest Competitions organised by clubs and newspapers to determine which player has gouged, sworn, punched, trodden and kicked less than anyone else in the team. Usually won by three-quarters.

BEST + FAIREST

Bidet Used in France for washing mud from boots after a game.

BIDET

Boots	More ceremonial than anything else. Nobody has been able to satisfactorily explain why Rugby can't be played in bare feet. Except that when players retire they would not have anything to (1) throw away, (2) burn or (3) store in a cupboard until they either go mouldy or the 4th XV finds itself short of players one afternoon.
Breakaway	Best-known of them is Rugby League.

C

Canadian Rugby	The worst thing that can happen to a Rugby player in Great Britain and Ireland, New Zealand, Australia, South Africa and France is to be transferred in his job to somewhere in the world other than these countries. There have been stories of these lost souls trying to

CANADIAN RUGBY

CHOICE OF ENDS

organise matches on the lower slopes of Mt Everest or on an island in the middle of the Zambesi River. The luckier ones have finished up in Canada, which is reportedly quite civilised, and they have organised their Rugby so well that Canada is now one of the better-known outposts of the game. One local custom if the ref isn't any good is to simply dump him on an iceberg and push him out to sea with just his law-book for company. This has led to a shortage of referees in Canada.

Cantankerous	Used by writers to describe battered old forwards who have played one season too many.
Caps	A cap, made of velvet and appropriately inscribed, is awarded on the occasion of a player's first appearance for his national team. At times they have been found to be too small for the swollen head for which they were intended. Most helpful when a player has to go cap-in-hand anywhere.
Captain	The player (1) whose father is chairman of selectors, or (2) whose mother washes the team jerseys each Saturday night.
Cauliflower Ears	A trade union membership card.
Centre	As in nerve-centre, he is supposed to be in the middle of all the action. However, if the forwards and halves decide to play what is commonly referred to as ten-man Rugby then he becomes a dead-centre.
Chairman of Selectors	The one who accepts blame for all the mistakes.
Choice of Ends	When the captain tries to decide whether to run uphill first or downhill.

Club Doctors

Ex-players who entered the medical profession and have returned to help the old club in an honorary capacity. The only problem is that they mostly become gynaecologists and obstetricians.

CLUB DOCTOR

GOOD NEWS~ YOU'RE NOT PREGNANT...

Coach

A man who walks into his house at the close of the Rugby season and his children say, 'Hullo mister, what's your name?' Coaches are seldom home, seldom happy and seldom satisfied.

Coin	Tossed in the air by the referee before the game starts to determine if the opposing captains have flexible neck muscles.
Corner Post	Hard to follow, as are so many things in Rugby. These posts don't have corners to them at all.

D

Dad	Soon after birth an infant boy first realises the problems ahead of him when a weeny pair of Rugby boots is deposited at the end of his cot, together with a copy of *Rugby Skills For The Beginner* and a small football. Dad will not rest from that day forth until you are capped for your country. The fact that you experience great difficulty making the reserves' bench for your house XV does not deter him. He knows you deserve much better than that and delights in telling the school principal so.
Day, Not Your	You have just been defeated 48–3, the team's champion centre three-quarter has broken down and there's no hot water in the dressing shed.
Dead-Ball Line	A succession of deceased footballs.
Defeat	When there are less officials and supporters in the dressing shed after the game than there were before it.

Disinterest

When the wingers hear the coach begin his team talk before the game with, 'OK lads, we're going to play it nice and tight today . . .'

DISINTEREST

Dive, Taking a An age-old ploy for gaining much-needed rest, or so the scrum-half can re-tie his loose bootlace, or the captain can figure out how to overcome the 42-point deficit. A designated player swoons like a Hollywood starlet at which point medical attendants rush onto the pitch and show their talents by treating him for a malady which doesn't exist. When the rest of the team is right to go again, he instantly recovers.

TAKING A DIVE

Dog

Usually black and nondescript. Runs onto the field just as the goal-kicker is lining up his shot at goal. If the crowd yells at him he has been known to relieve himself on the goal posts or even on the leg of the referee. No-one ever confesses to being his master. Runs off again after a few minutes. It's hard to convince non-Rugby people that this incident is not devised to provide added excitement to the game.

DOG

DROPKICK

Donnybrook	When players can't agree.
Dressing Shed	Where clothes and comfort are left behind.
Drop Kick	Should you miss the ball when attempting to punt it, this affords you a second chance after it hits the ground. If the ball passes accidentally between the goal posts you are awarded three points. Nobody ever tries it on purpose because it's too hard.
Drop-Out	The Rugby Blue from Oxford or Cambridge who winds up doing his thesis on violence on the Rugby field.
Dummy	(1) The act of shaping to throw a pass and then forgetting to do so. (2) Spat out by a player on the losing team who thinks success transcends enjoyment. (3) Your team-mate who has just dropped a pass with the goal line unguarded.
Dummy Scissors	A very tricky movement in which nobody quite knows what's happening except the player carrying the ball. Sometimes even he's not too sure. Forwards wisely stay clear of them.

E

Effort	What the coach always suggests at half-time is considerably lacking.
Ella Ella Ella	Hiccups which occur when watching Aussie Rugby.
Embarrassment	(1) You replace your torn shorts in mid-field and suddenly recall having forgotten to wear your supports underneath. (2) The opposition finally reaches a century of points and the game has to be stopped while the scoreboard attendant rushes off to get an extra batch of numbers.
End-of-Season Tour	A post-mortem and a strategy meeting for next season rolled into one.
Ex-Player	The pest with the stained club tie, bent nose and cauliflower ears who tells you later in the bar the correct way you should have done things out there today. Somewhere during the conversation he usually says, 'I remember a game back in '53 when . . .'
Extra	Extra lap of the oval. Usually reserved by coaches for tubby front-row forwards who have been found hiding in the loo during warm-up at training.

EMBARRASSMENT

F

Fair Catch The good-looking blonde you've picked up in the club-house after the game.

FAIR CATCH

False Teeth

Most forwards acquire them along the way, like grey hair and arthritic knees. Many wives and girlfriends have said they didn't know their men friends had them until they played Rugby (only on the pitch did they take on the appearance of gummy babies). Years ago, before an international match, the teams were to be introduced to a member of the Royal Family. It was suggested that those with false teeth should wear them for the occasion. Afterwards the teeth were collected in a bag. Officials could not have foreseen the confusion when the match was over, with forwards from both teams trying on various dentures until they found the right ones.

FALSE TEETH

Fijians	Rugby players who forget that the game is supposed to be designed for the players and not the spectators.
Five-Eighth	Does not play between the four-eighth and six-eighth as you might imagine. In fact, those two positions don't exist. (But in New Zealand they do have a first five-eighth and a second five-eighth!) Best just to call him outside-half, fly-half or 'hey you!'
Flanker	Flashy type of player. He stays well out on the flanks during the game but close to the female ones in the clubhouse later.
Football	The object which the laws determine is necessary for a game of Rugby, although some games have happily proceeded for several minutes before anyone noticed the ball was missing. Whoever makes them has a lot to answer for, as they never go in the intended direction. Often jaunty wingers find them as slippery as a cake of soap when there is an extra man in the back-line and the opposition is in grand disarray.
Forfeit	The excuse the opposing team offers when it (1) is short of players, (2) has forgotten the jerseys, (3) has caught sight of the size of your team's forwards or (4) has found the log-fire in the local much too warm to leave.
Foul Play	Informing the referee, just before kick-off, that one of your players is his bank manager.
Freezing	Temperature on the particular afternoon at Aberdeen or Invercargill when you've forgotten your gloves and overcoat.

FORFEIT

FULLBACK

French Rugby	A term which has come to describe anything which is undisciplined, volatile but somehow successful.
Frustration	A team looking around throughout half-time for a dry spot on the ground where they can sit.
Full-Back	A tipsy three-quarter.
Full-time, Or No-side	When the excuse for a few beers is over.
Future, Building For The	You haven't won a game all season.

G

Garryowen	A rugby club in Limerick, Ireland, with a great tradition. Full-backs wish it had never been founded, for it was from here that emerged 'The Garryowen'— the high-lofted punt supported by a rampaging forward pack. The eight forwards, all mean and snarling, arrive at the opposing full-back at precisely the moment he catches the ball. At this point it is wise for spectators to look away.
Genius	Your description of the opposing player who has just comprehensively beaten you on the outside and scored the match-winning try under the goal posts. *See* Quick.
Girlfriends	*See* Wives.

Goal Line	The line over which the opposition seems to have so little trouble crossing. You cannot reliably say whether their goal line even exists.
Goal Posts	Allegedly 5·6 metres apart, but any goal-kicker will tell you this is an absolute lie. They are much closer together than that.

GOALPOSTS

GROUNDSMAN

Grandstand	Where the experts are.
Grass	What is missing from the patch of ground where the largest forward from the opposing team has just tackled you, from behind, with the force of a runaway tank.
Grease	Applied to knees and eyebrows before a game to prevent scrapes and gashes, and thus also to the hand of the dignitary being introduced to you before the match.
Groundsman	The person who seems quite incapable of doing anything about the ridged, barren area of earth in the middle of the ground.
Grubber Kick	Although grub is a common Aussie word, meaning tucker, nosh, repast, pickings, nourishment or victuals, a grubber kick does not mean kicking-off straight after lunch. It is a kick which keeps close to the ground like a grub, providing the opposition with food for thought.
Guest Speaker	An ingenious way of occupying the time between dessert and coffee at annual dinners.

H

Haka	The dance the All Blacks perform before eating.
Half-Back	*See* Scrum-Half.
Half-Time	To allow spectators to visit the loo, or get another pint, or both.

31

HALFBACK

Headgear	Protective bonnet worn to prevent further hair from (1) falling out or (2) being pulled out.
Heaven	Boasts a wonderfully strong Rugby team, although a little light on front-row forwards.
Heavies	One of several names by which these people are known. Also called alickadoos, pests, necessary evils and officials. They stand at bars, drink Scotch and talk incessantly of how the standard of Rugby was ever so much better when they played. They materialise from nowhere at after-match functions, and dominate all the speeches. Something current players aspire NOT to be after they retire.
Hip Flask	Necessary part of Rugby watcher's equipment on a brisk winter's afternoon, as well as scarf, programme, mittens, sandwiches, loud-hailer and wife. The last item is optional.
Hooker	A sweaty, beastly little fellow, nevertheless having deep religious convictions about the game. Who else raises his arms to the Heavens each time he's about to become involved, before dropping devotedly to his knees?
Horrible	The feeling you get when you find yourself packing into the front-row against an opponent named Luigi and you realise he has eaten heaps of garlic for lunch.
Hurt	You are lying wounded on the ground and the coach leans down and says, 'It doesn't hurt, really . . .' But your ankle is possibly broken, and you would much prefer your mum's face than his looking down at you.

The fact that you are the goal-kicker and the team has just been awarded a penalty with the score at 3-all and only seconds to go has nothing at all to do with his casual dismissal of your injury.

HOOKER

Hush	The loud silence which occurs when (1) the ball has left the goal-kicker's boot and is heading for the goal-posts with the score 16-all and time running out and (2) the president announces that the club has again incurred a substantial loss for the year, the star fly-half has left them for another club and he has been re-elected for his 18th successive year in office.
Hyphen	When committeemen find it hard dispensing with their mother's maiden name.

I

Injury	The alternative to having a rest during a game.
Intemperate	The scene at 3 am when you've won the grand final.
Intercept	Other than pinching the bottom of the president's wife or allowing your son to play soccer, this is considered the most unsporting thing a Rugby player can do. Only those in the three-quarter line are ever guilty of it, which tends to make forwards think of themselves as having higher principles. Just when everything's going nicely and everyone's having a good time, one rotten sod will slip between two opposing players, catch the ball and run like blazes in the other direction.

INJURY

J

Jerseys	Dairy cows used for keeping the grass down on the playing field, where jersey-pulling takes place.
Jock	(1) A Scot who supports the game. (2) Another great supporter of the game. Keeps close contact with the most important parts of Rugby and every player would be left hanging loose without one.
Jones	Plays hooker for Wales. Also lock-forward, flanker, scrum-half and on the wing. *See* Williams.
Judiciary	The naughty lads wind up before members of the judiciary, who have usually failed to be elected to the club committee and thought this the next best thing. They listen to the fictitious ramblings of the culprit who has been sent from the field and then decide what to do with him. Sentences have included dancing with the president's wife at the next social.

K

Kicker	A fellow with a certain knack of propulsion who can neutralise the efforts of 15 other players.
Kick-off	The reason for the after-match festivities starts here. Constant moves to have this and the following 80 minutes dispensed with altogether have proved unsuccessful, as referees complain that they would feel unwanted.
Knock-On	The law states that a knock-on occurs after a player loses possession of the ball, or a player propels or strikes it with his hand or arm, or it strikes a player's hand or arm, and then travels forward. Actually, it's unjust discrimination against players with poor eyesight.

L

Lace	One of them inevitably breaks just as you're tying up your boots before the most important match of the season. You never have a spare.
Lansdowne Road	In Dublin. Not a place for cars, but where Rugby players run over each other.
Law Book	Something every spectator knows by heart and no referee has ever read.

League	A measure of length varying in different countries, the English land league being three statute miles and the nautical league nearly three and a half. Therefore, Rugby players can't understand why they must (1) do extra laps of the oval, (2) have a mouth-gargle or (3) report to the club secretary, if ever they mention the word.
Library	Every player worth his salt should have assembled a large collection of Rugby books by the time he ascends into the great pitch in the sky. They will range through topics like *How To Pass Your University Exams While Still Playing Rugby*, by Rodney Johnson MA (Hons) and *Unravelling The Mind of a Referee*, Volume II, by Professor Jeremy Smythe-Thompson, to more mundane subjects like *Lions Eaten by Springboks* (a comprehensive analysis of their most recent tour, full stats, vividly illustrated) by J. G. McK. Dobson, of the *Cardiff Bugle*.
Line-Out	A means of determining who is the best high jumper in each team while being held down, elbowed or bumped. Very difficult, especially as another player has to throw the ball hard at your left armpit at the same time.
Lions	When England, Ireland, Scotland and Wales want to make a tour at the same time they solve the problem simply by putting the names of all their international players in a hat, drawing out 30 names and sending them away as one team. Sometimes they play as bravely as lions, so they are called Lions. Other times they don't and Fleet Street calls them lots of other names.

Loose-Head
First identified in South Africa. A condition afflicting those who play in the front-row of the scrum and have one free arm. Only known cure is tightening, in which case the forward concerned becomes known as a tight-head.

LOOSE HEAD

M

Maul   A scrum or ruck where you are allowed to hold the ball in your hands, which leads you to being mauled.

MAUL

Meeting, Annual General	Once a year all the officials and players get together. The manager of the 3rd XV grumbles about the number of jerseys that keep getting pinched, the treasurer announces once more that the club is bankrupt, a complaint is heard about the brand of tea being used by the tea ladies and the president is re-elected unopposed once again.
Miss	The friendly cry of encouragement to the opposing team's goal-kicker as he moves in for a kick at goal.
Mound	Small pile of earth upon which kicker places the ball before attempting a goal or kick-off. He must be careful of (1) the ball toppling off the mound just as he is about to make contact, (2) the worm which crawls out from within the mound and onto the ball or (3) green shoots appearing if he takes too long.
Mouthguard	An uncomfortable piece of equipment, similar to a baby's dummy, which a player only learns about after losing several teeth.
Mud	Necessary for at least one game each winter.
Murrayfield	Murray used to be an undistinguished forward in the lower grades with Brothers Club in Brisbane. Other than the fact he once downed a pint of beer in 11·2 seconds there seems hardly any reason to mention him here. However, he says he has a cousin of the same name who has something important to do with Scottish Rugby.

MOUND

N

Nnooooo	The collective cry which goes up throughout the club-house when the meany who runs the bar calls out, 'Time gentlemen, please . . . last drinks'.
North Island	Half of what was left when New Zealand snapped in two. Largely a rural community, producing lambs for slaughter and Rugby teams whose opponents share their feeling.
Nose	The apparent target of every opposing boot and elbow.

O

Off-Side	The aroma from the opposite side of the scrum on a particularly hot afternoon.
Oranges	Quarters of these are eaten between halves. Old forwards eat the equivalent of an orchard during their career. Coaches have been known to inject them with vodka to (1) make them more tasty and (2) take the players' minds off the opposing team's 30-point lead.
Ordered Off	Only necessary when the hot water in the dressing sheds needs switching on before the game ends. The referee usually dispatches a forward on the errand and they never seem to go willingly.

Orthopaedic Surgeon The first people an old Rugby forward tells when he decides to retire are his orthopaedic surgeon, the club secretary and his wife, in that order.

P

Parents They run hysterically up and down the touch-line at junior Rugby matches behaving as they would not otherwise behave. Nevertheless they are necessary for the game's development.

PARENTS

Pass	Mostly thrown to good-looking birds after the game.
Patches	Worn on the jacket elbows to prevent beer on the clubhouse bar from soaking through.
Penalty Try	The only way of scoring a try when you haven't actually earned one. This is where Rugby enters the world of supernatural, for the referee has to gaze into his crystal ball and imagine what might have occurred had the player not had his progress interfered with. If you are a referee it's best not to award them. They cause trouble, and only mean you'll get pelted with eggs and tomatoes when leaving the field. When a penalty try appears to be 'on', you should quickly look away.
Physiotherapist	Person with whom a Rugby wife is certain her husband is having an affair.
Pinetree	Large carnivorous beast which once inhabited the North Island of New Zealand. Ate opposing forwards without so much as chewing them. Avoided capture for many years, but finally slowed down with age, allowing anthropologists to approach close enough to identify and name it. Was tagged Colineptus Earlingus Meads, or Pinetree for short.
Pontypool	Patch of land in Wales where they grow Rugby nuts by sprinkling them with coal-dust.
Pot	(1) As in 'Another pot, guv'nor, and don't take all day, the coach'll be back soon'. (2) When the fly-half seeks to 'have a pot' by kicking the ball between the posts after first dropping it to the ground. He usually misses.

President	Constantly makes reference in his speeches to his playing days, which nobody but himself seems to recall. Drinks Scotch and shakes hands with equal enthusiasm. Has been questioned by more than one player about his parentage and told that the club would get on a damned sight better without him. He ignores such talk.
Prop	Short support, hewn from timber or similar dense matter, upon which the hooker leans.

PROP

Pumas	Cougars or mountain lions. Also the name of Argentina's national team and like their namesakes prove troublesome at times.
Punt	The action of one of the three-quarters when all else fails. He hoofs the ball high in the air hoping it will (1) land on an opponent's head and knock him senseless or (2) bounce favourably so that he can chase and catch it, thus making a big name for himself. Usually the opposition gets it and simply returns it by the same method.

PUNT

Q

Query

When the skipper momentarily loses his senses and asks the referee why he penalised Tom Pudding for being off-side, when in fact he was lying in an off-side position but was at the same time being treated for a broken leg.

QUERY

Questionable	Referees sometimes make these decisions. Everybody thinks they're wrong but aren't game to say so.
Quick	Your description of the opposing player who has just comprehensively beaten you on the outside and scored the match-winning try under the goal posts. *See* Genius.

QUICK

R

Records

Rugby journals, books and magazines are full of all sorts of uninteresting statistical information about highest scores, lowest scores, number of goals kicked, successive wins, longest-serving presidents, fattest forwards and so forth. But many other pieces of information, far more interesting than these, go largely unrecorded. It is hoped this short list will go some way towards correcting the worst oversights.

MOST UNSPORTING GESTURE: To avoid sharing the ball with the opposition, forwards from the NSW Country team stuck the ball up the jersey of one of their kind while playing arch-rivals Sydney in 1975. The game continued for some minutes before the absence was noted. Country won 22–20.

WORST DISASTER: When Andrew McTavish, playing on the wing for St Jethrow's in an Aberdeen snowstorm, wandered away from his position and was never seen again.

LONGEST GAME: When the referee, Wing-Commander J. R. E. (Tiddles) Taylor-Horrocks, swallowed his whistle while the RAF Engineers were playing the Army Transport Wing and another could not be located until the following day. Another whistle that is.

MOST UNUSUAL DISMISSAL: Prop Jack (Granite) Nicholson was ordered off by a referee at Palmerston North in New Zealand after being caught smoking in the scrum. He blamed his mother, who wouldn't allow him to smoke at home or in public.

Referee Was given a whistle as a small boy and enjoys blowing it constantly. Interrupts what would otherwise be an exciting stoppage-free game of Rugby. Can recite Law 26 (3) (f) quicker than the date of his wife's birthday. Has no colour sense, sticking mostly to white co-ordinates. Has a very divisive effect on the game as half the people love him (the winners) and the other half think he's (1) blind, (2) a rotten cheat, (3) both.

REFEREE

Replacement   The cleanest-looking player on the field at the end of the match.

REPLACEMENT

Reserves' Bench	A panel of dejected souls.
Retirement	Must occur sooner or later, but it's remarkable how many times it takes place just as the youngster in the team below starts to impress the selectors.

RETIREMENT

Ruck	A disorganised scrum, where the forwards and referee are not entirely sure what's happening and in which the ball generally gets mislaid.
Rugby	A pastime of delirious enjoyment, much story-telling, plentiful drinking and occasional singing disturbed only by 80 minutes of often pointless endeavour on a strip of barren earth.
Rugger	The only persons allowed to use this as an alternative word for Rugby are those in direct succession to the Throne, or those who think they might be.

S

Scarf	Common piece of apparel, knitted in the club colours and used to identify those people who are not playing.
Scissors	(1) A movement where players criss-cross in order to confuse the opposition. (2) The instrument used to untangle knotted bootlaces after the game.
Scoreboard	The infernal apparatus at the edge of the ground which constantly reminds you just how many points you are behind.
Scrum-Half	Not eight players (which is half the scrum), but the little fellow called half (who is not half a man, but a full-grown man known as half) who feeds the scrum (which is 16 men). Like his name, he causes confusion.

Scrum Machine	An inert object.
Scrummage	A rather complex arrangement of arms and legs. In fact the only reason for its existence is so that the opposing front-rowers can exchange jokes. Sometimes, if they can't agree who's going to tell the first story, they fight.
Selectors	Men with pins who pick teams.

SELECTORS

Sevens, or Seven-a-Side	If the opposition doesn't turn up, you divide your team in half, make the one left over the ref and play sevens or seven-a-side. And if half your team doesn't turn up, you can divide what's left in half, make one the ref and play threes or three-a-side.
Shorts	In which a Rugby player spends many happy hours trying to get dirty and his poor mum many unhappy hours trying to get clean. Manufactured with care so that at least one pair rips during every International Match.
Shove	The forward momentum used in scrummaging and crowded bars.
Singing	An integral part of Rugby, ranging from the soothing lullaby of a mother singing to her infant in an effort to drown the noise of the Rugby International father is watching on television, to the thunderous sounds of 60 000 Welshmen clearing their throats at the same International.
Sir	The name players call a referee to his face, as in 'Please sir, is that law in the book or did you just make it up?' Behind his back they call him other names.
Skin	Donations of this are made by Rugby players to all groundsmen, who consider it excellent fertiliser.
Springbok	A species of antelope in danger of extinction.
South Island	The other half of New Zealand. *See* North Island.
Stab Kick	A kick (1) keeping low to the ground with the purpose of going beyond the attacking line and (2) as in stab-in-the-dark. Even the kicker doesn't know where it's headed.

Stitches   The state the captain lapses into when you announce that you're sick and tired of playing front-row and forthwith want to be considered for the wing.

STITCHES

Studs	The reasons for their use have never been fully documented. (1) They are generally thought to have been placed on the underside of players' boots to make it easier to avoid the chewing gum on dressing-room floors. (2) Obviously of great assistance to groundsmen, as they furrow the soil ready for the seeding of next summer's cricket pitch. Also, mother's immediate thought when told by daughter that she is going to a party given by the local Rugby team.
Suggestions	They are always being generously passed on to the referee, as in, 'Hey ref, why don't ya get ya bleedin' eyes tested . . .'
Summer	That time of the year when kids recognise their Rugby-playing father more readily. The lawn gets mowed, the back fence fixed and the lounge room painted.
Sunday Morning	You wake and wish you had not consumed that last pint of beer the night before. Of course your state of health has nothing to do with the 17 or 18 pints before that. Your head and body ache in unison and you wish Sundays could be eliminated from the week.

SUGGESTIONS

T

Tackle	A part of the game in which you have no particular interest. It involves trying to provide an obstacle for an opponent to fall over.
Team Lists	Those strips of paper displayed before each match showing who is playing in which team. Only the bravest start by looking at the 1st XV. The quickest way of locating your name is to start with the Extra A 111s and work upwards.
Team Photographs	Needed at the close of each season to cover the damp patches on the clubhouse walls. The day they're due to be taken usually coincides with the captain coming down with measles or the champion fly-half wearing odd socks to training.
Team Talk	(1) Delaying tactics by the coach to stop his players getting to the pub before closing-time. (2) The alternative to training if it's too cold outside. (3) When the coach tries to explain what he wanted done in the last match and why it wasn't. (4) When the president calls the players together to inform them that the local publican has complained about their behaviour and moves a motion that they shift to another pub.
Thought	Behind every excuse in Rugby. The winger says 'Gosh skipper, I thought he was going to run straight ahead instead of using footwork like Fred Astaire and finishing up behind me . . .' Or the drawling prop who has just conceded a penalty at 12-all with only minutes left

conceded a penalty at 12-all with only minutes left says, 'I'm sorry fellas, but I haven't touch a footy for a coupla years and thought nobody would mind if I touched it in the scrum just this once . . .'

THOUGHT

Throw-In	You throw your wallet, car keys and false teeth into a bag held by the team manager for safe-keeping and hope you get all or some of them back after the game.
Ties	Necessary piece of clothing, although nobody ever seems to buy them, only give them away. Committee-men are particularly fond of them, as they cover the naked midriff where the bottom shirt button parts from the small aperture in which it is supposed to be inserted.

Tight-Head	The result of a loose-head being tightened.
Timekeeper	The man who waits until the visiting team is only one point behind and busily pressing your goal line before deciding to ring the full-time bell.
Toast	(1) Anyone or anything used as a reason to start the drinking at Rugby dinners or (2) when the opposition are 30 points ahead they are said to have you 'on toast'.

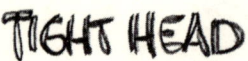

TIGHT HEAD

Touch	A line separating the players from the spectators. Kickers hardly ever find it when they want to and too often find it when they don't.

TOUCH

Touch-In-Goal	When your team-mate snips you for a fiver while you're waiting in the in-goal area for a kick to be taken.
Trainer	A contemporary slave-driver whose task is to get teams at least remotely fit for the beginning of the season. Relishes pain and suffering. Players retaliate by deflating his car tyres and hiding his whip.

Training	When your team practises all the secret moves it never gets to use during a match.
Trophies	Are indispensible to the game of Rugby and awarded at the end of each season to various deserving people, including the club member who spent most money at the bar, the player who attended most training sessions and the girlfriend or wife who didn't miss a match. The fact she cannot remember a single score doesn't count.

TROPHIES

Try	There are two kinds of tries (1) What your dear old mum tells you to do as you walk out the garden gate, 'Try not to get your shorts too dirty, Billy . . .' and (2) what your coach says to you in the dressing shed, 'Try your bleedin' 'arts out there today lads . . . and don't come back if ya lose'.
Tweed	A twilled woollen cloth which Rugby players use in their jackets to identify themselves from non-Rugby types.
Twickenham (Twickers)	Famous UK habitat of birds, either streaking, or being consumed with champers in the car-park.

U

Ughhh	The escaping sound as opposing front-rows thump down against one another in the scrum. Also their dialogue together after the game.
University	That team whose shorts are a little longer, socks a little higher and birds better-looking.
Unkind	Words the coach uses to you in the dressing shed when the game's over. You plead that you couldn't help it if the opposing winger crossed for six tries. The sun was in your eyes.

| **Unwise** | The decision to remain on the ground near the ball when the All Blacks decide it is theirs for the taking. Stone monuments have been erected to this sort of hero. |

UNWISE

Up-and-Under	If you're a spectator and it starts raining, common sense tells you to get up and under shelter. An up-and-under on the field is the same as a Garryowen. It's best to get clear of them, too.
Upright	The fly-half who calls the ref's attention to the fact that the pass he has just thrown was slightly forward.
Utility Player	Not much good in any position.

V

Valleys	More commonly known as The Valleys. An area of South Wales smeared with coal-dust where men from towns and villages with odd-sounding names drink beer, work, sing and play Rugby in equal proportions.
Vice-Captain	In charge of the team's activities after dark.
Vice-President	The fellow who longs to be president, so he can get the key to the liquor cabinet in the committee room.
Victory	A player realises it has happened only when he finds the dressing shed more crowded than when he left it.

VICTORY

W

Wales	They have never been beaten at Rugby, although other teams have been known to score more points.
Wallabies	Smallish kangaroos which spend their life jumping all over the place. Despite their size, big men in black and even Lions have occasionally been frightened by them.
Water	(1) Magic liquid rubbed onto injuries during a game which instantly cures broken limbs, bleeding noses and bruised joints. (2) What the club president uses sparingly in his Scotch.
Weak	The feeling when you're about to pack into the first scrum of the game against a rival prop twice your size, who possesses no teeth, has a nose bent like an elbow and constantly makes threatening noises. Your other prop steadfastly refuses to change positions with you, adding, 'Any last words for the family . . .?'
Whistle	The most persecuted implement in Rugby, as the referee is always being told to (1) throw it away, (2) swallow it or (3) put it in a most uncomfortable place.
Williams	Plays for Wales where Jones doesn't. *See* Jones.
William Webb Ellis	Had it not been for young Billy's impetuosity, lawns would be tended, dogs washed, sinks unclogged, gardens weeded and rooms painted on Saturday afternoons. A tablet set in the wall surrounding the playing fields at Rugby School perpetuates his memory in the following terms: 'This stone commemorates the exploit

of W. W. Ellis who, with a fine disregard for the rules of football as played in his time, first took the ball in his arms and ran with it thus originating the distinctive feature of the Rugby game. A.D. 1823.' William Webb Ellis subsequently entered the Church and became the incumbent at St Clement's Dane in The Strand in London, but there is no record of him ever retaining an active interest in the game he so inspiringly founded. Just think what he missed.

Wind	Can be quite distracting at times in rucks, mauls and scrums.
Wingers	Speedy players who run away from the hard stuff and into the score-line.

Wisdom	Dating the ugly daughter of the chairman of selectors.
Wives	Are extremely grateful to William Webb Ellis for inventing a way of allowing them to knit for at least 80 minutes without being disturbed.
Women's Rugby	Started in the United States (which you might have expected). Now growing there in popularity. The wives and girlfriends of players thought that if you can't beat 'em then join 'em. The husband or boyfriend who wore old pantyhose under his shorts to prevent grazing now has to buy his own.
Writers	Sometimes they are celebrated old players with arthritic knees, but mostly they were hidden away on the wing of their school's 3rd XV. They delight in telling current players how they ought to play the game.

X

X-Ray	The favourite pastime of club doctors is sending players off to hospital for X-rays. They have been known to elope with pretty radiographers.

X-RAY

Y

Yaaamuuug	Quaint Aussie expression to suggest that the referee should perhaps be better informed on the laws of the game.
Yanks	Have taken to Rugby like politicians to a microphone. Early problems caused by Texans wanting to wear their ten-gallon hats, six-shooters and spurs during a game and the Red Indians in the team wanting to take scalps if they won have now almost been abolished.

Z

Zero	Your team's score when you haven't done very well.
Zzzzzzzzzzz	Sounds emanating from outside the fence when the referee is trying to demonstrate to the players just how much he knows about the laws.